Dark Fathers

and other poems

Dark Fathers
and other poems

by

David Anthony Sam

Cover design by Shay Culligan

Cover art by Cynthia Ann Price

ISBN: 978-1-950462-46-9

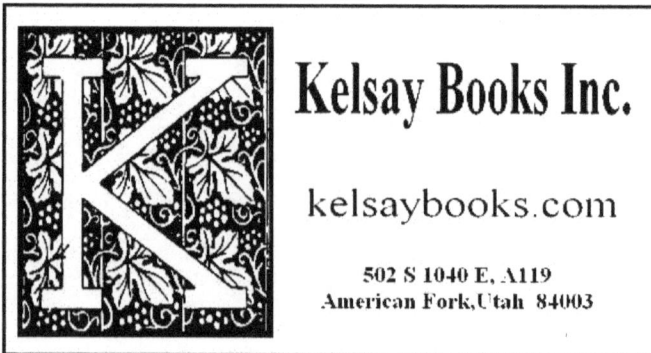

Kelsay Books Inc.

kelsaybooks.com

502 S 1040 E, A119
American Fork, Utah 84003

For my father, Tony, who became so much lighter with the years—
and for his father, Elias, whom I knew only in dark images.

And always, for Linda, my loving partner in life.

Acknowledgments

My thanks to the editors of the following journals for having previously published poems from this collection:

Aji Magazine: "Anchises"

Arlington Literary Review: "Dark Fathers"

The Birds We Piled Loosely: "Bad Dreams"

Blue Unicorn: "Hungry Inside"

Crosswinds Poetry Journal: "An Old Chaos (Sunday Morning)"

Door = Jar: "River and Father"

Gravel: A Literary Journal: "Genetic Geologies"

Haunted Waters Press – *From the Depths:* "Climbing the Red-Dog
    Road"

Inwood Indiana Review: "Pileated"

The Magnolia Review: "October 25, 2001"

Poetry Quarterly: "First and Last" (2018 Rebecca Lard Award),
    "My Yellow Season"

Red Queen Literary Magazine: "Lineage"

The Summerset Review: "Eloquence," "This Weaving"

The Write Place at the Write Time: "Betrayals," "Harrowing
    Hallow's Evening"

Yellow Chair Review: "Cutting Deeper"

Contents

About the Author

Alleles

Genetic Memory

My saliva contains much memory
                  that Ancestry.com
        has parsed into strains of history—
        of parents and grandparents and distant more
        mixing fluids with lust and dreams,
                   depending me
                   from a tree
that grows from peasant roots
watered with time.

Tribes and farmers
worked flesh and soil
in continents of passing years
and lives.
Tsars and Nazis, Ottomans and Caesars
conquered with rapine and sword
and left their mark in helixes
that are more eternal than any form
they take in flesh   or memory.

An ocean of difference
travelled four in stinking holds,
dividing me from certain knowledge
of the names I would evoke
but rest in silence.

I wear a mix of nomenclatures
the way the English dictionary
is made of broken   tongues
reknitted in mongrel tapestry.

My paternal grandmother's surname
is the first that I was called.

It carries the remains of alleles
fractured
                             by an ocean—
                                  written
with blood and hunger.

I am
        a memory of tending horses,
        namesake of a shepherd,
        grandson of peasant peddlers
        a Samaritan elevated beyond dry olive fields,
        a Sami.

And so I grow a speculative tree
        with brittle leaves
        and spittle speaking genealogy.

        fractured by an ocean
                writing memory in my flesh

as water writes in sand.

Dark Fathers

I know my father's father
only as he fades
in one browning snapshot
taken two years before
his lungs breathed final blood.

He glares from history
with a hawk's black eyes,
suspicious that the camera
might reveal his failures,
a peddler with nothing left to sell.

He is a scorn of choices,
of golden Syrian dreams
dying on American concrete.
He left only his image
fading with the photopaper

into the sorrow that sometimes
wore my father's face
and ghosts now in my mirror—
as dark fathers fade
into my dissolving image.

The Syrian (for my grandfather)

His dark brow and darker eyes
wearied of peddling hope
across foreign streets.

His English, gutturaled
with Arabic phonemes,
made it a hard sell at Cerberus doorways
eyed by Hungarians, Poles, and Germans.

In poor streets of Safita and Homs
he'd heard the promises of gold
in some America
that did not exist except in glitters of deceit.

Now he walked snowed streets
from West Newton to Pittsburgh,
drinking his profit as fast as the wind
drove ice
into his stranger face,
dragging a cart
clattering emptiness in pots and promises.

Lineage

A shadow of howls wakes
the cry of the dark grandfather,
coal black for eyes
and lupine hunger—

Your dreams were
the images in a stream
fragmenting moonlight
with brittle waves.

I flow from you, grandfather,
in a haze of cigarette smoke
and the incantations of wine
spilled into a drunken snowbank.

You damned the good Samaritans
who brought you home
to my grandmother and my father
and were damned in return.

I hear you cry the night
in the empty space
where God once stood
full of mere prayers.

What did you have left to sell
from your peddler's cart
when the earth spoke
its soil welcome?

Climbing the Red-Dog Road

The tires growl gravel
in unmusical rattle,
as the blue Ford sedan
slowly climbs the hairpins.
I ride the rear seat
breathing my father's cigarette
smoke and weary anger.

Grandpa's house was high
above the Monongahela,
and although we could
drive way around the back
of the hill on paved roads,
my father insisted on
challenging the red-dog meander
of the steep hillside.
He mutters in first gear
as the car whines like a dog.

The green trees and brush
close in on the two ruts
that mark the way,
branches striking out
as if to ward off flies.
My mother navigates
the silence. My sisters sleep.

How I hate the cigarette smoke,
the bleary exhaustion
of trying to please my father,
the stale weakness
of my mother before his fury.

How I dream myself
an alien trapped in
this flesh of blue steel.
I feel bile rise with nausea
and pray for the car to stop
its endless weaving.

And then it did, and they
were all sudden gone
with the smoky dream
that leaves me woozy,
rising at first dawn's light
on a distant cold morning

Returning Home, Late

The sun falls too quickly behind
western Pennsylvania hills,
even in the high summertime.

From the backseat of the '52 blue
Ford sedan, hazed in a gray smoke
from my father's glowing Pall Malls,

riding beside my sleeping sister,
returning home to McKeesport
from my grandmother's house

in West Newton, or from my
mother's parents' hilltop farm
in Monongahela,

in vibrating lateness of the dark,
I would lean my head against
the half-open window,

both to breathe clean air and
to eye the clear stars in a night.
I would wonder at houselights

like stars in the black heaven
of western Pennsylvania hills.
On the crests of rolling roads,

farmhouses appeared as shadows
opaquing the stars behind them.
Some sent dim yellow glows

through windows, and I dreamed
into each window, each light,
burning in the late night as

an astronomer studies each star
through vestiges of light to know
what worlds were there.

The front seat was drenched
in my parent's silence. Could I
find refuge in an alien planet

like the one I read in Pratt,
a home for a foreigner
alien in his own family?

Silences kept a cold burning
like the stars in the night above
the hills of western Pennsylvania.

Then we rolled downhill into
a dark valley, where there were
no stars, no houselights, just sleep.

Pallettes and Steel

He worked the welding torch,
flaming sparks against the black
faceplate of his mask, dripping
fast-congealing metal stars
onto the oil-smeared floor.

The war was over, his leg,
broken against the telephone pole
in the motorcycle accident, mostly
healed, though the steel plate ached
inside when the weather changed.

He was a silent, sometimes sullen
worker and a fierce and silent leader
who sang like Dean Martin
and glared like Jeff Chandler.
His men disliked his sometimes

stiff coldness, but most were so
loyal they would follow him into
the bowels of the broken machinery
of the assembly line, all exiting
greased black and weary.

Decades passed with twelve-hour
days, seven-day weeks. His children
matured without him noticing.
And then—just before his 55th birthday—
his heart stopped twice.

They pounded his chest to wake him,
broke open his breast so his heart
could be reprieved. He prayed to live
long enough to screw the company,
long enough to meet his children again.

Now he works to liberate the colors
held within his fingers, free the images
he dreamed, remembered and invented
through the brush of paint to canvas
board. He must free himself from living

only black or white. The acrylic aromas
intoxicate him better than
the daily sips of sad whiskey
drinking sadness at Lakeview Tavern.
The war was over. His life unbroken.

He works the brush and pallet,
reflecting hues against the mask
of his hard face, dripping fast-congealing
memories of warm Italy and lost suns
onto the oil-blessed canvas.

Bad Dreams

Dark within the dream
I lick memories
from raw soil

bend quaking sounds
into noise that
semblances you

Sin is born
from the fire
of wanting what isn't

Black teeth speak
mist
in the crevices

Unsure unseeing
something seems missing
from the not-knowing

With what regrets
my father
forgot to go home

Betrayals

The wind howls storm.
It means nothing.
It means nothing that
I have been betrayed
and the storm rains me.
The two do not connect.
Not really. But I rage
that he has stolen
my soul with false love.

The dark mist,
the deep rumbling
suit me fine. Now,
it's better to rant a storm
all out of proportion
than murder love.
Being a poet is
a smaller crime.

He was my father.
Now he is mist
sprayed against
filthy glass.
It means nothing.
It means everything.

Cutting Deeper

I will use a blade now,
to shave, no longer
an electric razor.
My facial hair
too grizzled, too coarse.
My face too creviced.
My face too like my father's
who knew love
only as a hard, thin edge
of glinting blue steel
scraping across his cheek.

Taken Together

Taken together,
the death of an old dog,
the cancer of an old cat,
the dry end of winter,
and the dying heart of a father,
all mean no more than the bluest ice.

Resurrection is for
earth-born flowers
and star-borne heroes.
For us, there is the waiting,
the withering of dreams,
and a glass of sherry before darkness.

Hungry Inside

Hungry inside, my father eats
his way out of my flesh.
When he is free of me,
all that is left of him within
is a rough, brown scab,
like a surgeon's wound,
along the left of my abdomen.

Hungry outside, my father tries
to cut back in. He cannot.
Beneath the scab, the scar is pale,
lifeless, but firm and tough.
It lets nothing back within—
his hunger unable to do more
than scratch at my flesh.

I love him as I love each wound—
They are so hungry
to be still inside me.
But I remove him from my flesh
as I remove the scab,
stand back, admire the whitened scar,
paled, nerveless, hardened.

Sometimes there is a little blood.

Dream Before Open Heart

In dream, the telephone bleeps,
I answer, and my father speaks.

"Where am I?" I don't know.
But I understand that he has died.

We waited too long to call each other.
We waited too long to speak.

"Where am I?" Now his voice
comes to me as the recording you get

when you have dialed a wrong number,
disconnected syllables, female.

I hang up the receiver. But the voice
is in my ears with its Where am I.

I turn over, wake up, feel my
sinuses drain from left to right

across my face. I stare at the blank
wall, dark latticed with moon white.

"Where are you?" I mouth to the wall.
Moonlight pretends its pale answer.

Quadruple Bypass

In the morning, while I walked
along the highway sacrificing
the sunlight and the warm April
breeze to my shadow and my
distant thoughts, I suddenly knew
that the heart is just a muscle
waiting to die. And I felt anger
in my armpit, and the loss of feeling
in my fingers. My breath stopped up,
my forehead wore sweat like
the dew that beaded on the new
maple buds. Traffic whirled by.
But I heard a roaring in my ears
that drowned out all other sounds.
Just as suddenly, I awoke from
the pain in my chest and saw
that I had become my father,
he who cannot walk near traffic
from fear the wind will drown him.

Waiting the Silence

How is it, waiting as you do for each
unsteady throbbing of your heart
on the edge of something dark and quiet?
You paint with a shaky hand what
you see with limiting vision, knowing
you are closer to ultimate blindness.
You pedal that stationary bicycle
so you can be reassured by its steady
thumping in your ears, and for one
moment draw a quick young breath again.

I could offer you a year or two of mine
with false bravado. It's better instead
for me to feel the shortness of January
days, the fragility of weak winter sunlight,
the solemnity of long winter shadows,
the cold wind drying my face, numbing
my fingers. Then, take up my body and walk
across the angry distance between us,
hold you closely for one brief long while.

Passage

Dear father, hungry for your once youth, now finding
peace as your flesh sags weary from the bones your heart
betrayed by stopping up with January snow, it is a gift
of Christmas that you are able, for the first time now,
to tell me that you love me before leaving south
for Florida and the risk we should never meet again.

Now I am the age you were when we broke away from
each other, each betrayed by the other not being
what was expected—now I am humbled by my
childless state, aware as I have never been before
how wonderful and fearsome it must have been for you
to have a son so unlike and then so very like yourself.

Now, it is a gift of Christmas that we can embrace,
two men on the edge of two abysses, forgiven and
forgiving, one heading south for warmth and the strange
birds of Florida, one remaining with snow and those
very stubborn birds of every thin Michigan December.

First and Last

First, there is just darkness.
A long pause as the heart dies.
See, he breathes, but with difficulty.

I remember the time he kicked my dog
from the newly painted porch.
I thought he was a son of a bitch.

Then, years later, he gently cradled
the same dog in his arms
as the vet injected it with death.

I found out just today the dog
had brain cancer. For 27 years
he's kept the knowledge from me.

But he can't keep death's knowledge
from himself. Between each faltering,
the half-dead heart still pumps.

Wondering if that last thud in him
is the last thud he will feel
last, just before the darkness.

And when the machines fail,
the new therapies don't work,
the operations cannot open heart's blood:

In the end there is just darkness.
I can see it in the furrows
plowed into his forehead.

My father is afraid now.
I would cradle him in my arms
if it would make the knowledge go away.

Morality

My yellow dog shivers his age,
finds the heating vent, curls
his nose into arthritic hip.

My father sleeps with one ear
awake to the thick thuds
of his weakening heart.

My memory of a day in December
eighteen years ago grows dimmer
than memories of novels I have read.

Winter is miserly with snow,
and I am grateful for the frost
that silvers the grays and browns.

Doppelganger

On the dream edge of cold,
I start awake, the dreaming
seeking its daylight suicide.

All desire will have refrozen
into an unsleep of February
howling crystal sculpting wind.

The blue snowbank near
the frozen river wakes my
want to speak cold daylight.

Why voice such light of day
when dreams would snuggle
an unreal comfort of warmth?

For when I awake, my father
will have died, his lungs filled with
words he never could breathe.

How can I know I still live
lying here in cold shadows,
his angry silence beside me

sleeping like a lover I'd
abandoned eighteen years ago
when first I failed to sleep.

My Yellow Season

Ghosts of my yellow dog
and my younger self still run
the back alleys together,
kicking up snow or puddled water,
attached by a leash in a wild dance.
He grew arthritic-hipped, could not
stand by himself, let alone run.
The vet gave him a lethal dose
of anesthetic. Now, I dose myself

with memory. My father wore
staples over his heart from
the quadruple bypass he had.
He had to be careful lifting things.
I remember when he'd lift me on
his shoulders, and I'd wrap
my arms around his forehead
and his thick black hair, and
we'd play horse and rider in the yard.

He shrank beside me, his white
head inches below mine where
once we were the same height.
He diminished until it was
a good time to die. October
has killed much: my yellow dog,
my pretty illusions about a hued
immortality of leaves, my father.
Harvest means a dying time.

Thus it is a good time to touch
the earth, now that the soil
is cool, the leaves rich in rotting

aromas, the apples invigorating
in drunken fumes. But I have
killed my yellow dog, and my
sere autumn self knows there
are fewer springs, waiting after
the drifts of snow that wear me.

October 25, 2001, at 6:45pm

Silence—
a paper sign on a gray door
"Room R2"
in plain red paper
and plainer black letters
and an open doorway—

a whiteness of hospital bed
and hospital sheets—
the stillness of this body
mouth wide to hold
the intubation tube—
the infinity—

his coal black eyes
covered with gauze,
cloth coins for Chiron—
the belly swollen
like a small hill
of red clay—

the empty flesh
and vacant clothing—
the surprise
of being fatherless—
and, instead of emptiness,
an overwhelming knowing—

it is as it is
as it must be
as it will be
forever
in Room R2
and hereafter—

Atonements

Memorial

We buried you today.
I think you would have
not disliked the service
too much, it being short
without that preaching
righteousness that kept
you from pew and pulpit.
Elvis and Dean Martin
sang in baritones with
range to touch us all
from death, immortal
in recordings we sold
together in the store
between our quarrels.
You would have been
embarrassed by the praise
but also glowed, head
down, slight smile near
smirk, closer to a word
like love that had these
last years found expression
there. How principled, how
modest, how prideful, how
stubborn, how Pyrrhic,
how selfish, how dark,
and finally how weightless
you now become in silence.
Now—what are you?
A large man in a small
town, you had made
a difference. Eulogies
were spoken. Hundreds
came to hear. The mute

testimony of an awkward
girl, now grown into
an awkward woman, read
by a stranger from badly
typed script said what
we all were hearing when
the casket graveled into
unforgiving earth: We
want you for more days.
We want your painter's
hand to draw more colors
from this gray, gray world.
We want to see your ghost
again walk these streets.
We want to hear your
voice sing "That's Amore"
as we watch the moon
rise weakly in our sky.

From Virgil

I come to the lake, Avernus, with
solemn steps through its dark-edged rocks.
Slow mists ballet across the black water,
slowly boiling, a memory of the lava
that once glowed thick red in the crater.
The moon, which had lit my way up here,
has sunk now behind the volcano's
sharp crest. Darkness fills the deep
crater: silence, windlessness, and me.

I have come to the lake, Avernus, to talk
with my father, to let his words bathe me,
to bring an offering of green branches
to Spring herself, still captive for the season
below. My father is dead, but not deadened.
His words are like the lakewater, dark,
moving slowly, aware of time as the lake
knows of time, not flowing, not caring.
His words are not words, but speak
to me still–of a gray future, and of my death.
And I hear without words, without ears.

Then, as a dream, I am back
on the shore of Avernus, where no
life lives or grows; and the quaking below
is the door being closed on my father,
on my touching pure time, on my wordlessly
knowing what no life can know.

I go from the lake called Avernus,
enlightened by darkness, aware of time
again as the river knows time, still caring,
still in clear and changing water,

no longer beneath a black unmoving lake.
But I will return to Avernus, when
the river I am finds its blackness.
And my father will open his arms to me.
And Dis may at last let me smile
in the spring and in the branches I've given.

The Right Oracles

The fathers are all dead,
their prayers silenced.
Now we stand
as elder orphans,
parents to ourselves with
generative empty hands.

We are children grown
wiser than we are,
asking the mute oracles
to protect with right
words and gestures
what our ineptness lost.

What the fathers taught
was partial, incomplete,
wisdom worn away
by a fiercer sun,
harsher winds and rains,
erosion of sedimentary faith.

So we children now
stand as the latest elders,
hungry for the old hand
on the shoulder,
the spectral touch
that fails to heal.

Apparitions

Fathers who have died
try their hand as ghosts,
naming
from the grave
their sons, still,
asking for proof of love
still, asking for the acceptance
they never had themselves
as sons, nor ever could give
as fathers, even from
the grave,
still.

Autumn, Ashes, Elegies

We are made to feel the beauty
and the terror of the world.
Designed, mud up, from the rock
and lava, the boiling seas,
we feel love and fear for
this life, this world.

A moment before sunrise,
the east sky beginning blue,
stripes of pink clouds like veins
radiating from a hidden sun
presage—what?—a bloody morning,
a death, a birth? All
come every day. We applaud,
we mourn, we laugh, we are
one with the bloody world.

We make the sky and clouds
metaphors of meaning
when the sky is mere refraction.
the clouds reflection,
and the blood just ashes.
Like a fire, our life, our
consciousness, exists in energy,
the momentary combination.

All heat, fuel, air,
we burn, we burn,
we become the ash
and a burst of light
before darkness.

The Fathers' Dreams

Rise in a cold dry season, come
awake with winter over seeds
that have faith within them,
grow in a small corner under
clouds that burn in radioactive
dreams, and become a no-more-child
when the century is ending.

Dreams and memories: A Father's
War, a burning of the planet,
murder most foul made assembly
line style (Henry Ford was a Fascist
pacifist). When they wake, then
become a baby at the breast,
hungry for what was withheld.

Dreams of wars in black & white,
manufactured in John Wayne Hollywood.
Korea, Pork Chop Hill, preparation
for a son's war, mildewing
in Asian jungles, Dienbenphu,
France left, here we come.
John Wayne singing Barry Sadler.

Dreams in color on the 6 o'clock
news, choppers, M-16's, Puff,
DMZ, B-52's, flashing yellow
clouds, gleaming in Tet, body
bags, glistening black. Hello,
son's war, withheld, in time.
Hello Vietnam. Number 162.

Too many dreams, impotently
draining the young blood from
old veterans. And all non-veterans,
huddled around their history,
recalling their numbers, 162,
and the day they became too old
for a draft in limbo. Free, but old.

Suddenly, the Wall comes tumbling
down, Russian soldiers visiting,
will sing war no more, suddenly,
the Father's War coming an end.
Are the clouds free? Glowing
only with sunlight, not angry dreams,
not the hunger still withheld?

Enter the thunder. Shouting freedom.
Eastern Europe aflow in streets
awash with banners, not of blood.
Watch in silence. Polish relatives
somewhere in the stream, wanting,
thundering, freedom. It's a winter,
seeds with faith within them.

Enter thunder, Syrian brothers,
Arab sisters, war by barrel bombs,
war of gases melting eyes,
distant relatives somewhere
in the bloody stream, wanting,
thundering freedom. But it's
desert winter, the seeds are dying.

Emigrations

I am surprised by morning
with a clarity of fog like
fading photographs praying
echoes of Syria.

How do I paint suffering
into the singing of birds
and the quiet wind
that still scents of concrete?

There is a father's land,
and here is my birthplace,
and the colors of each
hue themselves into my sight.

Two immigrants came,
stayed, made a history.
What remained behind dies
daily in unpaintable ruin.

Genetic Geologies

Sated with pasts of red clay and coal,
quartz sand and pale gray mud,
I live on histories not my own:
Huddling in dark holds of reeking ships
that toss a cargo of flesh with each wave—
Peddling dreams and dry goods in snow
drinking the wine of self-pity and hope—
Arguments shouting Polish over boiling
chicken and perogies while a fire raged
in drunken fireplace reddening the night.
I fail to write the truths of these memories
encoded in my breath and blood, my
flesh layered in genetic geologies that
I try to parse like the folds of the earth
after the eons have uplifted mountains.

Photos Lying Apart

He, a youth of 22, standing before
a Roman fountain, standing between
two Roman beauties, coal black hair,
olive face and black eyes,
a smile almost a sneer, almost shy,
almost in love with Italy
and the beauty on each arm.

She, posed almost coquettishly,
proud in her nurse cadet uniform,
one leg so, hip thrust so,
smiling with that smile of a woman
not so far from being a shy girl.

Their first car, a used 1942 Chevy,
dark gray or black—the young couple
embracing each other, leaning against
the car. He proud of his ownership
(in both), a cocky tilt of his head,
her body nestled in against his,
laughing with her face and eyes.

Now there are four,
a toddler and an infant
between them,
a family sitting on a hillside,
still in black and white.
Hers a weary smile for the camera.
His, no effort to smile at all,
impatient with the posing.

The only posed portrait as a family:
Father sitting, brooding, black hair

sprinkling with gray, heavy brow
almost shadowing the eyes
that narrow in on a dark future.
She sitting with the baby,
a weak and formal smile.
The gangly eldest, suffering
teenage hatred for his posture
and his very existence.
The second-born, pig-tailed,
a bit apart from the rest, leaning inwards.

Only in an accident of children's marriage
or grandchild's birthday does long
estrangement close a moment
to capture them together now, sitting
at either end of crowds and long rooms.
Here he has gained a mane of white hair,
a pregnant belly, an ease he had not had
when young and arrogant.
Here she sits by the flames in the fireplace,
her face still with the complexion
of rose cheeks and slight smile,
but with eyes that brood the distance.

His last picture, wan, old, tired,
resigned smile, head close to his son's,
shorter now than his son, knowing the cold—

and her last photo, lying in a hospice bed,
smiling weakly as the tabby curls
against her near useless legs—

images as far apart each from the other
as eternity can make them.

Journaling

As I have this journey
as you have none now
so I will write what
steps I take missteps
I make old memories
real or ones new sewn
I make this habit here
perhaps each day so
if behind my shoulder
you can read from your
redisintegration into
starstuff you can know
how I have slipped into
the suit jacket of your
body a copy of the poem
you held close and see
each word hereafter as
reaching for you where
I am coming fast as this
brief living my goodbye

Born of Decembers

For my winter always,
I promise a million dreams,
a million hopes, a million years
of love and memory
for the dead of my life,
my father, my friends, my lost
past selves.

For my winter never,
I know I will never
hold again the dead of my life
in my flesh-laden arms,
my father, my friends, my lost
dreams of perfect
wholeness.

For my winter wonder
I breathe, I stand, I see,
I feel. I laugh, I taste.
I still love,
I still have
someone to touch, to love
before the long coldness.

For my winter sorrow
I feel the cold songs
falling in snow,
crystallized in my frozen
singing, chapped, cracked lips
saying old words,
my past worlds.

For my first fatherless winter,
I stand to see the bright sun
skimming off the blue diamonds
of snowbanks, souls
of my father, my friends,
my past lives, still the words,
my words—still.

The Dark Painting

The memory of you fades
as your face recedes
into the place where
all lost things go.
It becomes harder
to draw your image
from the lagoon of mind.

I resist the forgetting:
how you smiled, how
you frowned, how
your hair went from coal
as black as veins in
Pennsylvania
to silver, then to white
like Michigan winter drifts.

I resist the forgetting:
the muscle clench
in the sharp jaw line,
the dark eyes like
those of a circling hawk
or of your mother;
the mischievous grin
when you teased or
the solemn smirk
of your dry humor.

But without photos,
your image grows dark.
And even the photos begin
to fade, colors washing
into a stale sepia,

black and white
brittling into shadows,
photos falling from their
certain places in old black-
paged albums, the glue of
old corners loosing with time.

Lost somewhere in the great
sea, somewhere the currents
may draw together,
strange attractor—photos,
images, memories
form somehow again
like oils from your palette,
painting out your face
from the darkness, ancient
gods drawing you
into a constellation of
unknown stars.

Morning at Shaving Mirror

The mirror said "Father" to the dull scrape
of morning across my bearded face.
He seemed weary, and a little older
than I'd remembered him.

"Why the disguise?" I asked.
"I may despise you sometimes,
but I've never tried harder to
love someone than I have you."

The mirror mumble-lipped back at me.
I took my glasses from my face
and baptized it with hot water,
trying to remove the image.

It stuck to me like life hanging
onto the final seconds. "Father,"
mirror speaks. I listen.
Beware what you love in the morning.

At the Edge of Stars

This beautiful tenuous planet
hangs onto the rim of its galaxy,
hangs desperately onto the life
that animates it, gives it knowing.

How fragile, little, how quick
to fall into the dark chaos around.
How soon my father left me.
How soon my mother must follow.

How beautiful and tenuous my hold
on life is here in quicksilver world.

Iconoclasm

Steadily, the temple falls
gray, as Sam-son I lose some
hair, my forehead rising
with the years in ironic
simile to the wrinkles of time
furrowed in my brow.
My belly is paunched
in profile by too much
gravity weighing me
down without my humor.
My strength was always
in my jawbone, and my
words bray dusty silence.
I have little appetite now
but much hunger is in me.
My eyes rheum over in
the ancient mirror, going
blind as stones fall and
my chains link forever
with the fathers who have
aged, fled, and withered
before me. There is freedom
in the breaking of old gods.

My Father's Paintings

Two of his paintings suspend themselves
from the walls of our newest home—
two acryliced faces, a Vietnamese woman,
a Bolivian man, both peasants with eyes averted,
neither confronting you with clear sight.

These faces have hung near me for five decades.
The old woman, a face of the despair of war.
The old man, a mask of wariness and rage.
As unknown as their subjects are to me,
they are as knowable as my father ever was.

Painted with an intuitive brush by hands long-
stained black with oils from the machines
he tended at the factory, these portraits
are the autobiography he never wrote.
His silence solidified now in brushstrokes.

Beneath the paint, you can just see traces
drawn in delicate and hidden pencil
of a life he'd horizoned for himself
drawn deep beneath furrows of resignation.
Almost too late to image his forgiveness,

he had become the paintings that graced him
with wry smile and not the phantoms of his past.

An Old Chaos (Sunday Morning)

It is Sunday and I try praying—
not just because it is Sunday,
but because you are not here.
The words I whisper come out
as silence, unmeaningful,
like the mystery of Russian
Father Kreta spoke at the Blessed
Virgin Mary, while I gaped at
gold stars on the blue ceiling.
Communion meant kneeling
and kissing the gilded saints
on the holy books, eating dry
bread floating like a crouton
in the watery bitter wine.
You were never with us then—
mom told us you were agnostic,
which meant you feared death
too much to hope for any God.

Now I faithfully commune with
your memory, your deep voice
echoing in elegies of "Swinging
on a Star" and bitter whiffs
of beer on your crooked smile.
Prayers come out of me in
questions of the cold dead:
Did you find love in painting
acrylic faces and landscapes?
Did you dance again after leaving
all of us for younger hope?
Did you hear my anger like a prayer
when you crossed the wide water
without sound?

I have believed that we must burn
ourselves with manufactured meaning.
That might be just more watery
wine with a few floating crumbs
drifting in the hunger of stillness.
I hope selfishly that you still
flow in some dark energy,
like the hidden currents in
the muddy Youghiogheny.
Was the open O of your mouth
an epiphany—or simply the shape
carved by the intubation tube?
Regardless, you flow here
in my transient river as it
drifts with silence towards
the open prayer of ocean.

Harrowing Hallows' Evening

I am sorry but I cannot believe you
in your total absence from everywhere
except in resurrections of dreams.

I am sorry that I witnessed your body
gaping mouthed from loosing soul
to its escape wherever it goes now.

I am sorry that I touched a cold shell
that was not you. Although you had once
been so cold and rigid in your living,

you were not so when you fell back
into your death chair while playing
with the children in your store.

I am sorry it has been seven years
that I have hoped to reawaken you
to your deep voice and lighter smiles.

Today, Halloween, your favorite
of holidays, I look into the masks
of every ringer of our door and hope

to see your black eyes filled with sparks
of laughter, pretending that you do not
now wear death as your ever costume.

I am sorry that, as I go to sleep, I still
am trying to let you go, so you can lay
the path I have to follow in my own way.

If you can, make the way clear, as once
you did, holding my hand along dark
streets, showing me the tricks of shadows

on older All Saints Eves when spirits
rose and memories were made. I am
sorry that I still jump at such old ghosts.

Paternal Summers

i

Each turning spade of soil
loams sweet memory
of a long garden sloped
to a Pennsylvania Hill:
My father's red shoulders
glowing raw as he stoops,
weeds among the rocks,
piles the unwanted green
heat wilted into brown.
He wears a warpaint of black loam
wheelbarrowed from green woods,
his dark face sweat-streaked—
like the muddy spring creek—
as his staid shaman visage.
He greens peas to sweet snap.
He spades potatoes out of dark soil
mined like Pennsylvania anthracite.
He vines tomatoes into thick heaviness
and walks corn rows as tall as he
while winds blow silk
to stalks rustling and pregnant.
The hillside nourishes his dark love
for his family as his black eyes
close over his dark need.

ii

A decade turns like spaded soil.
My father angry hoes gray Michigan clay
while my mother bangs meals
from dented pots,
divorce ripening the garden
split between them. Sunlight
between the dying Chinese elms
defines garden limits while
food rots uncooked in the fridge.
Heart plaques thick, muscles
starve and pump blood
where no love lives while
flesh still needs, skin reddens
in the angry sun within.
He turns, he weeds,
no doctor can prescribe the green
he seeks to grow within the rows
among the dappled shadows.
He burns in furious sun, harvests
hate by shovelfuls, feeding
the mulch to something pure,
dark love nourishing his family
while his black eyes close
and his need harvests winter.

iii

A Virginia spring turns me
spadeful and unangered
in some late redemption
where I mulch the past
into a soil memoriam for him.
From black loam composted
from decay and red clay,
I harvest darkness to something
purer, nourishing my family,
grace of fruition, the still air
miraging with angry heat.
Blackness streaks sweat
in rivers on my face,
At peace, I wear the shaman's mask
my father left lying in the sun.

This Weaving

The eating of the pear
remains of summer
where I may pray
by speaking to the dead.

The pear replies
with juice and terrible
sweetness.
The dead retort
with their customary
silence.

Except some dreams
permit them words
while pears in dreams
stay tasteless.

My journal nightly
speaks dear to those
I remember best
within my genes:
My father's voice
sometimes comes between
my lips and tongue.
My mother's eyes
sometimes confuse
the mist of morning mirror.

The other dead must
depend on the fragility
of patterns sewn loosely
in the contexts of my brain.
It seems that memory

reweaves itself
from daylight and
those transitory fibers
of my sleep.

The pear decides to share
its wealth by oozing
sweetness to my hand.

The dead cannot decide,
their sweetness lost
to unfathomed taste
like the savor of
the fog that wakes
me morning.

In the Dream

In the dream, my word of love
Lazarused my father from his death.

In the dream, he lay, corpsed to
a hospital bed, as he had lain
thirteen years ago, his mouth
still gaping from the frenzied
efforts to pump his dead lungs
and silent heart back into motion.

In the dream, he lay still attached
to the flat-lined meter.
I bent over, called him, and told
him I loved him, as I had done
some four years ago. But
in the dream, he awoke to my words,
sat up, became himself, an even
younger self than his final 78 years.

In the dream, he walked from
the hospital into the bright blue day.

In the dream, love could resurrect
the lost, could rebody the dead.

In the dream, my mourning could
be turned into bright cocoon.

It was a Christian dream, but
hunger is no savior–and so
my father never rose again.

Petits Madeleine

A broken bottle of Aqua Velva
on the drugstore floor—
and I am twelve again, trailing
the oakmoss traces left by my father
as he exited the bathroom for
his trudge to the factory in Romulus.

Stale ash in the park firepit
resurrected by a summer drizzle—
and I am twenty-two in the foothills
near Bend, watching a fire I'd built
into a nightmare smolder
before the chill morning hike.

Marsh rose along Stony Creek
windborne and beeborne—
and I am sixty, trailing the traces
of my years, identifying the scents
of the hopes I had discovered
left along the footpath I'd forgotten.

Anchises

I heaved my father's corpse
into the singing stream
that flows into the cave
which opens its mouth
just once in every year.
His corpse was weighted with
my needs and fears, my childhood
wants of the tall man
who had made me.
His corpse was weighted with
stones of adolescent anger and
with the bulky satchels
of an adult disappointed
in the terrible heaviness
of a too mortal man discovered
by his too mortal son.

Every year thereafter, I came
to stand beside the shining stream
to look again at the closed cave.
And every year thereafter, I counted
the days of his life that had overlapped
the days of my own.
And every year thereafter, I dwelt
in the heaviness of his
leaving me until
steadily the darkness of the tall father
shadowed smaller and smaller
like the time I realized I had grown
taller than he—or

that he had shrunk before me.
And every year thereafter, I felt the bittersweet
of love unweighing itself of
the anger of mortality.

But on the tenth anniversary of his leaving,
when the cavern opened its annual mouth,
my father's corpse
danced lightly from the water,
gilded from mists of spirit,
golden with levity as he
sublimated like the ice of winter
directly sunned into the vapors of spring.

River and Father

I dream my father
dark and angry
in a thunderhead
weeping what was never
and can never be his.

I once tasted
the sweet meat
of the date that grew
along our river
that drifts now with debris.

My father refused
the sweetness of the water
and tasted only bitter
tears and blood
in the meat of the date.

I have become
his eyes and tongue,
become his anger
in my step and in
the words I fail to say.

He has moved
beyond the waves
that echo bank to bank.
He speaks the river
in my dreams.

Face Above Water

In this the month
of the brilliant dying,
the Rapidan River is painted
by the yellow and orange
of the green cessation
along its wandering banks.

The low cloud of unknowing
hangs above the water,
weaving in and out of the trees.
The water runs rapid
from late October rains high
in the Blue Ridge.

It is another anniversary
of the end of your being.
And, when clouds drift so low,
they ghost the holy face
that is supposed to be
our last and lasting sight.

I do not believe in more
than the sailing of dead leaves
the way the current goes
as it travels towards the Bay
to join eternal water in the sea.
I stop to watch the going.

Standing beside the self
that obscures my own way,
I hunger to become the unknown
knowing of these clouds,
to see you rise in the flow
of this patternless vapor.

I speak the names of seasons
as a cold wind buffets me
from a source in the mountains.
The unknowing clouds disperse
into the realistic sunlight.
Water blurs with yellow, orange.

Eloquence

In the stillness of misunderstanding,
the ocean echoes
a harmony of waves' journey.

The soul your past speaks
is the wander of waves,
the whisper of water.

You are becoming the sand
of a mountain's erasure
drawn down to the shore.

The ocean sings
no meaning, no birth,
no death, in sines of movement—

breaking across its own
sculpture, an art
of deep forgiveness.

Pileated

His hand is in the rapid hammering
as if his touch still carpentered my world,
shaping with router and band saw
the wood that grew from the black humus.
His eye is in the black seeing centered
in this flying aimed at fulfilling hunger
from what tunnels or bores into the trees,
just as his sight straightened the cut with
right angles measured by steel square.
His voice is in the near-mad laughter
of being freed into feathers, unknowing
forever in the reincarnation of spring
from migrations beyond these woods,
like the gentleness his wit became when
he had moved three times past death.
I sit on our porch each morning, waiting
his return from the night as a shadow
flying from nothing into the something
of my seeing, hearing. His presence
is fantastic, like the brief half-memory
of last night's dream before the sunlight
chases it into the very darkest green.

Navigation by Dream

His large hand
encompassed my small,

his hand hard
mine soft as youth.

We walked a dream,
a forested ridge,

watched by a fragile yearling
contained by mist.

He gathered wild onion
and wild carrot for stew.

He browned the beef
in a bubbling of butter,

then cooked in a blackened pot
I stirred with expectation.

We sat above the covered bridge
above the muddy river

and ate from flat aluminum plates
with stainless steel spoons.

He pointed to the Milky Way
and the bear and Polaris

and said this was the guiding light
he hadn't found in church,

the way he navigated,
the way his father had not found.

He never showed me the photo
of his dark father, dead before my birth.

Instead he held my hand
as we stumbled down the slag heap

that smoked beside the river
that smolders still in dream.

About the Author

Born in Pennsylvania, David Anthony Sam is the proud grandson of peasant immigrants from Poland and Syria. For much of his life, he lived and worked in the Detroit area, graduating from Eastern Michigan University (BA, MA) and Michigan State (Ph.D.). He lives now in Virginia with his wife and life partner, Linda. Sam's poetry has appeared in over 90 journals and publications and his poem, "First and Last," won the 2018 Rebecca Lard Award. He has five published collections including Final Inventory (Prolific Press 2018) and Finite to Fail: Poems after Dickinson, the 2016 Grand Prize winner of the GFT Press Chapbook Contest. He currently teaches creative writing at Germanna Community College, from where he retired as President in 2017. He serves as Vice President for the North Central Region on the Board of the Virginia Poetry Society.

Other books by David Anthony Sam

Dark Land, White Light (1974, 2014) Dark Land Publishing

Memories in Clay, Dreams of Wolves (2014) Dark Land Publishing

Early in the Day (2015) Dark Land Publishing

Finite to Fail: Poems after Dickinson (2017) GFT Publishing

Final Inventory (2018) Prolific Press

www.ingramcontent.com/pod-product-compliance
Lightning Source LLC
Chambersburg PA
CBHW022203080426
42734CB00006B/555